PP 234

T3-ALT-298

432
W66
1989

HEMIDEMISEMIQUAVERS

. . . and other such things

A Concise Guide to Music Notation

For Gloria Wood

HEMIDEMISEMIQUAVERS
. . . and other such things

A Concise Guide to Music Notation

Colorado Christian University
Library
180 S. Garrison
Lakewood, Colorado 80226

Dale Wood

The Heritage Music Press
Dayton, Ohio

EDITORIAL CONSULTANTS

Larry Pugh
Dorothy Wells
Eugene McCluskey
Lyle Ditzler

PRODUCTION

Unitype, Rohnert Park, California
Typography

Sun Ho Kim, Seoul Music Co., Seoul, Korea
Music Engraving

The Lorenz Corporation, Dayton, Ohio
Photolithography

©MCMLXXXIX The Heritage Music Press
501 East Third Street
Dayton, Ohio 45401-0802

This book, or parts thereof, may not be reproduced in any form whatsoever
without written permission of the publisher.

Library of Congress Catalog Card Number 88-83507
ISBN 0-89328-103-4

All Rights Reserved
Printed in the United States of America

INTRODUCTION

This book is about the little squiggles and curlicues which most musicians love to read but hate to write. Properly assembled, these symbols become a universal language which is understood throughout the civilized world: music notation.

The art of music notation began in Greece some 3,000 years ago. Letters of the Greek alphabet were used to designate tones. As the system developed, some letters were inverted and altered, new musical alphabets were introduced, but the methods became unwieldy. With the development of plainchant in the Middle Ages, symbols eventually replaced the Greek letters. One can envision how the symbols evolved and became more elaborate as Christian monks hand-copied the Gregorian chants of the church.

Many of the symbols used in modern notation were in use 300 years ago. As the evolutionary process continues, traditional practices which are no longer pragmatic must be discarded in favor of sensible reform. Library shelves are lined with sizeable volumes on the subject of music notation but many are so broad in their scope that they are cumbersome for quick reference. There has long been a need for a concise volume which addresses the subject in succinct terms.

Here then is **Hemidemisemiquavers*... and other such things,** a reference guide on music grammar and the elusive art of music notation. It covers notational rules which are absolute and those which are flexible. It casts aside notational practices which have outlived their original purpose but retains those which cannot be improved upon. The rules and examples given here reflect the best principles of modern usage.

Unless one notates music on a regular basis, it is difficult to remember the myriad rules of how to do everything correctly. The performing musician readily comprehends a musical passage on the printed page but may have difficulty writing out a similar passage in his own manuscript. Even the professional music notator must occasionally ponder the proper way to set down certain elements which are used infrequently, for the rules of music notation escape the memory quickly.

---

*Hemidemisemiquaver: a sixty-fourth note.
Also called *quadruple-croche* (French), *semibiscroma* (Italian), *Vierundsechzigstel* or *Vierundsechzigstelnote* (German), *semifusa* (Spanish).

Music notation is rarely taught at any classroom level today. The teacher of harmony or theory usually evaluates only the subject matter and rarely corrects the syntax of how the student actually notated the exercise, error-filled as it may be. The student may become proficient in the rules of composition while the manuscript remains the work of an amateur.

Poor manuscript may suffice in the classroom but rarely will an amateurish manuscript be suitable for performance or possible publication. Music publishers do not employ copyists to do what is considered the composer's work. The responsibility of a music editor is usually limited to the final rectification of a near-perfect manuscript.

It is assumed that the reader is familiar with the fundamental elements of music notation and can fluently read a printed score. The reader must also be able to draw these basic symbols legibly.

CONTENTS

1

BASIC MANUSCRIPT TECHNIQUES

MUSIC MANUSCRIPT PAPER

Manuscript paper is available in a variety of sizes with varying numbers of staves imprinted. The folio format (a sheet folded in the middle, creating two leaves) is usually printed with staff lines on both sides, providing four manuscript pages. *Folio sheets are not recommended for most applications.* The copyist will frequently wind up with unused attached pages or make a serious copying error on a page which cannot be singly discarded. It is also a nuisance to photocopy pages which must constantly be unfolded.

Single sheets of manuscript paper are recommended. Staves are usually printed on both sides of single sheets but experienced copyists use only one side in the event a page must be discarded because of a major error. *Manuscript paper with preprinted braces or clef signs should be avoided* since these symbols often do not match the prerequisite of the job at hand.

Select a page size for expedient photocopying. All photocopiers use 8½ x 11″ paper stock and music manuscript sheets are available in this size. While many photocopiers will reduce an oversized image to fit 8½ x 11″ stock, the notation will also be diminished and can become difficult to read.

The number of printed staves on a page is important. Keep in mind the number of staves required to form complete systems for different copying jobs, thus avoiding unwanted blank staves on the page. Space *between* staves should be wide enough to accommodate any texts for vocal music.

Imprinted staff lines should be well-spaced. If the spacing between lines of the staff is too wide, needless time is spent drawing oversize note-heads and symbols.

Test the paper stock for erasability. Preprinted staff lines should withstand heavy erasing and the paper fibers should not easily disintegrate.

PENCIL OR INK?

Photocopiers have antiquated the requirement for manuscripts written in ink. A pencil with soft lead will reproduce with ink-like quality on a good photocopier. Experiment with drafting pencils and select a lead which erases cleanly and does not smudge. The novice will undoubtedly call the eraser his most useful tool.

Poor quality copies will result if the notator fails to use a pencil with soft, dark lead or if lines and symbols have not been drawn darkly enough. Augmentation dots and ledger lines should be well-defined marks or they may drop out when photocopied.

A little trial and error will ultimately result in first-rate manuscript copies. Once the art of pencil technique has been mastered, the copyist will concur that the tedium of pen and ink work is indeed a thing of the past.

OTHER HELPFUL TOOLS

A **straightedge** is indispensable for ruling bar lines and beams neatly. A ruler about 6″ long is easy to handle and transparent plastic ensures accurate placement of ruled lines. Many copyists use a straightedge almost constantly to guide the pencil while drawing the straight lines of accidentals, stems and beams. A proficient copyist can move the ruler and pencil with lightning-like speed and even the novice will soon discover that the moments spent in drawing perfectly straight lines will improve the manuscript quality immeasurably.

A **French curve** is a drafting instrument which can also come in handy to draw long ties and slurs with accuracy and neatness. Though not essential, the use of a French curve in certain instances can enhance the quality of the manuscript work. Stores which sell drafting supplies have French curves available in a wide variety of shapes. Select one with long, gentle curves; other templates on the instrument will provide shorter arcs which are useful.

DRAWING MUSIC SYMBOLS

Notators should not attempt to match every curlicue of the rather ornate contours common to engraved music symbols. Clean, well-defined pencil strokes in the obvious general shape of curved symbols is preferred. The finished manuscript should be a neat blueprint—not a calligraphic masterpiece.

The most glaring error found in manuscript is the notator's failure to consistently distinguish between the thick and thin lines common to the majority of music symbols. All manuscript work should reflect this thick/thin variance, particularly in accidentals and beams. Beams must be heavy, dark lines and two or more repeated pencil strokes are usually required. It should be emphasized that *some* of the ornate symbols found in engraved scores need not be copied in manuscript with special attention to the thick/thin lines. Detailed calligraphy is not required for clef signs, for example. Simply conform to the overall shape and size of the engraved forms of these symbols.

Notators get the best results in drawing thick/thin lines when the pencil tip is slightly dull. Pencils with soft lead can be slightly rotated to control the blunt side of the tip for drawing thicker lines.

NOTE-HEADS should be drawn with a slightly oval shape, *not round*. They should be centered on the line or space and they should completely fill their required space between lines (or equivalent space) on the staff.

1. BASIC MANUSCRIPT TECHNIQUES

STEMS must *connect* with all note-heads in perfectly straight, vertical lines, best drawn with a straightedge.

ACCIDENTALS must be precisely centered on the lines or spaces they represent, immediately to the left of corresponding note-heads and not separated by any considerable space.

TEXTS AND DIRECTIVES should always be neatly printed in upper- and lower-case letters. Typewritten texts are preferred, but when hand-written, never carelessly intermix capital letters with lower case. Vocal texts must have hyphens correctly inserted between every syllable of every word. Insertion of hyphens should never be guesswork; consult a dictionary or word guide whenever in doubt.

2
SYSTEMS, BRACES AND BRACKETS

When using a single staff for vocal or instrumental parts, no connecting line, bracket or brace should be used at the left margin. The staff lines should remain "open" with the clef sign being the first symbol:

CORRECT   **INCORRECT**

SYSTEM: When two or more staves are joined together, the unit is called a system.[*] The staves connected in a system are then read simultaneously rather than one at a time. To form a system, a connecting line is first drawn through and between the staves at the left margin:

↑ **CONNECTING LINE**

To visually organize the staves, a brace or bracket is added to link two or more staves together. Both of these symbols are used for a similar purpose but *the brace and bracket are not interchangeable.*

BRACE: The large, curved brace is used only for keyboard and harp music. The brace is placed in the margin, just to the left of the connecting line:

↑ **BRACE: USED FOR KEYBOARD AND HARP**

Brace as used for Organ

---

[*]A system is sometimes erroneously called a "score." For clarity, *score* should be reserved to mean the written form of a musical composition.

2. SYSTEMS, BRACES AND BRACKETS

Small braces may be used between the staves in organ music to indicate that both hands play on the same manual (keyboard). The specific manual name may be shown to the immediate left of this small brace:

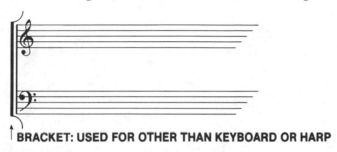

BRACKET: To organize a system for other than keyboard or harp music, a straight bracket is drawn in the margin, just to the left of the connecting line:

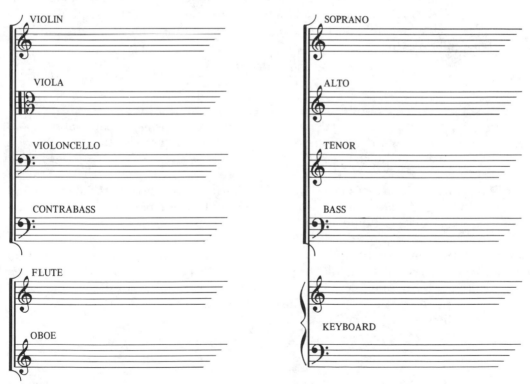

BRACKET: USED FOR OTHER THAN KEYBOARD OR HARP

A bracket may be extended to connect many staves of vocal parts or *like* instruments:

Bracket as used to connect *like* instruments   Bracket as used to connect choral staves

Note: The connecting line joins *all* of the staves together at the left margin to form a system. Bar lines, however, do not necessarily follow this same pattern. They are more commonly drawn only through the staff lines and not between them. (See Chapter 6: Bar Lines.)

3
CLEFS AND STAFF EXTENSIONS

Of the many clef signs that have evolved over the centuries, only three are used today in modern notation:

 G-clef (also called the treble clef): Used for the highest register. Its position on the staff is fixed with the open loop of this symbol encompassing the second line to indicate **g.**

Alto

Tenor
C-clef (alto or tenor clef): Used for the middle register. This clef sign is movable and the center of the symbol indicates middle **c.** When placed on the third line, it is called the alto clef; when positioned on the fourth line it is called the tenor clef. Since the symbol is somewhat difficult to draw, it takes on slightly different forms in manuscript:

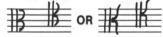

 F-clef (commonly called the bass clef): Used for the lowest register. Its position on the staff is fixed with the two dots always placed above and below the fourth line, indicating that the note written on this degree of the staff is **f.**

Prior to 1750, all three clef signs were used in various positions on the staff to avoid ledger lines. Today, only the C-clef assumes more than one position, identifying the alto and tenor clefs as noted above.

The C-clef is never employed in keyboard or vocal music today, nor is it used exclusively by any instrument. Its primary application is to eliminate excessive ledger lines in instrumental parts. The alto clef is commonly used for viola when necessary; the tenor clef is used for the high range of contrabass, cello, bassoon, and tenor trombone.

3. CLEFS AND STAFF EXTENSIONS

LEDGER LINES

Notes that exceed the compass of the staff require the use of ledger lines. These are short lines which extend the degrees of the staff upward or downward as required. **Ledger lines are always drawn *exactly* the same distance apart as the regular staff lines and they should be slightly longer than the note-heads themselves.** Precise spacing and alignment of ledger lines is critical to ensure accurate reading:

OCTAVE SIGNS

When consecutive notes remain above or below the staff, reading can be facilitated with the use of octave signs instead of ledger lines. Octave signs placed above the treble staff or below the bass staff transpose written notes to different octaves as described below:

> *8va* or *8* (Italian abbreviation of *all' ottava*, meaning *at the octave*) **is used above the staff (*only in the treble clef*)** to indicate that notes are to be played one octave higher than written. The abbreviation may stand alone over a single note or chord, but it is always followed by a broken line over extended passages. The line is terminated with a down-stroke immediately beyond the conclusion of the *ottava* passage:

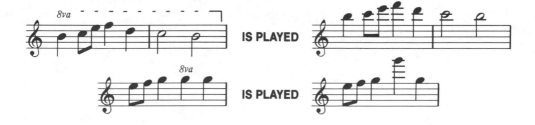

> *8va* **is used beneath the staff (*only in the bass clef*)** to indicate that the notes are to be played one octave lower than written. The broken line is then ended with an upstroke:

The word *loco* (meaning "in place") may be inserted at the conclusion of an *8va* passage to indicate that the notes are to be played where written. The use is somewhat redundant since the termination of the broken line signifies the end of the octave transposition.

15ma or *15* (Italian abbreviation of *quindicesima,* indicating the interval of a fifteenth, i.e., the double octave) **is used only above the treble staff** to indicate that the notes are to be played two octaves higher than written. *16va* and *16ma* are mistakenly used but a two-octave interval is a *fifteenth* and should be correctly abbreviated *15ma.*

Single notes to be played *in* octaves are marked with a different abbreviation. ***Coll' 8va*** or ***coll' 8*** (sometimes written ***col***), meaning "with the octave," is used to specify that the octave is to be *added* and not transposed. A solid line (rather than the broken line) is used for extended passages to be played in octaves:

Placed above the treble staff, *coll' 8* indicates that the octave above the written notes is added. When *coll' 8* is written beneath the bass staff, the octave is added below the written notes.

4
KEY SIGNATURES

Key signatures must be placed directly after the clef sign at the beginning of every staff. The correct placement of sharps and flats in the key signature must be strictly observed:

When using the alto or tenor clef, key signatures must be shifted as one unit and repositioned accordingly.

KEY CHANGES

A change in key may be inserted anywhere within a composition immediately following a light double bar line:

It is not necessary to cancel an existing key signature with natural signs before inserting a new one. The insertion of a light double bar line automatically cancels any previous key signature:

Exception: Natural signs should be used (following the light double bar line) when indicating the new key of C major or A minor:

When a change in key signature occurs at the end of a system, the new signature is inserted following the light double bar line (as usual) but the staff lines must remain open at the right margin. The new signature also appears at the beginning of the next system:

5

TIME SIGNATURES

A time signature is composed of two digits placed one above the other on the staff. The lower digit indicates the unit of measurement (quarter note, half note, etc.) and the upper digit indicates the number of such units in a measure:

$$\frac{4}{4} \quad \frac{3}{4} \quad \frac{6}{8}$$

] = Number of units per measure
] = Unit of measurement, i.e., quarter note, eighth note, etc.

Time signatures are never separated on the staff with a virgule (/) as used in fractional numbers. (A time signature written within the body of printed text may be written as 4/4, 3/4, etc., simply because of typesetting limitations.)

Time and *meter* need clarification for discussion. Meter is the recurring pattern of pulses or beats. These recurring beats are set off between bar lines to form a measure; the first beat of a measure receives a primary stress. **Meter is indicated by the time signature.** For example:

$$\frac{2}{4}$$

This signature is referred to as "two-four *time*" or defined as duple *meter.*

Theoretically, there are over 90 possible time signatures but for practical reasons, only the most common are used here as examples.

Simple Meters

Duple meter   = two units to the measure $(\frac{2}{2}, \frac{2}{4}, \frac{2}{8})$
Triple meter   = three units to the measure $(\frac{3}{2}, \frac{3}{4}, \frac{3}{8})$
Quadruple meter   = four units to the measure $(\frac{4}{2}, \frac{4}{4}, \frac{4}{8})$

The symbols C and ϕ (mistakenly called "common time" and "cut time") are ambiguous and their use is not recommended. The precise, two-digit time signatures are preferable.

Compound Meters

(Compound meters are simple meters multiplied by three)
Compound duple meter: $\frac{6}{2}, \frac{6}{4}, \frac{6}{8}$
Compound triple meter: $\frac{9}{4}, \frac{9}{8}$
Compound quadruple meter: $\frac{12}{4}, \frac{12}{8}, \frac{12}{16}$

Imperfect Meters

Imperfect meters are not equally divisible by two or three and include time signatures such as $\frac{5}{8}, \frac{5}{4}, \frac{7}{8}, \frac{7}{4}$, etc.

PLACEMENT OF TIME SIGNATURES

A time signature should appear at the beginning of a composition *on all staves*, immediately following the key signature:

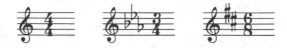

Regularly alternating meters are shown by a double time signature with a plus sign (+) between the two:

Combined meters with irregular alternation may be shown with double time signatures, the second set off in parentheses:

For clarity, cue notes should be inserted over the time signature and above the staff to indicate if note values are to remain constant (shown above left) or if the beat is to remain constant (shown above right).

Single-digit time signatures have been introduced in contemporary music when meters constantly change. The single digit is centered over the middle line of the staff and it indicates the number of units within each measure:

Some editions with constantly-changing meters use no time signatures whatsoever. This practice is dubious because the performer will undoubtedly pencil them in anyway.

5. TIME SIGNATURES

CHANGE OF METER WITHIN A COMPOSITION

Whenever the meter changes within a composition, the new time signature is shown on all staves immediately following a *single* bar line within the first measure of change. If a meter change occurs in the first measure of a new system, the time signature must also be shown at the end of the previous system and the staves left open:

END OF SYSTEM ↑

*Traditionally, a light double bar line was used before every change of time signature. This is **not** recommended in modern notation; a single bar line is preferred.*

Meter changes can sometimes lead to confusion over whether note values change or remain constant. It is advisable to use cue notes over such changes in time signature (above the top staff of each instrumental or vocal part) to clearly indicate the transition:

6

BAR LINES

BAR LINES (the vertical lines drawn completely through the staff) are used to mark off measures and visually organize the meter in music. Unlike the initial connecting line drawn at the beginning of each system, *bar lines are not necessarily drawn unbroken **between** every staff in the system*. The following rules should be observed:

Keyboard Instruments *(except organ)* **and Harp:** Bar lines continue unbroken between the two staves.

Organ: Bar lines continue unbroken between the two staves for the manuals but the pedal staff is barred independently.

Vocal Music: Each vocal staff must be barred independently to avoid interfering with the placement of the text.

Conductor Scores: Bar lines are drawn unbroken between the staves for each instrumental *choir* (woodwinds, strings, etc.) but are broken between unrelated groupings.

Although commonly seen in manuscript, an unbroken bar line should never connect all the staves at the end of each system.

Note: Bar lines are *not* placed directly at the end of systems where there is a change of key or time signature. When these changes occur at the end of a line, the new key signature or time signature becomes the final symbol on the staff. The bar line is drawn immediately before the signature change as always and the staff lines remain "open" at the end of the system:

6. BAR LINES

LIGHT DOUBLE BAR LINES are used to mark the end of a section or placed before a change in key signature (but not *time* signature):

FINAL DOUBLE BAR LINE (two vertical lines, the second being much heavier) is used only at the end of a movement or composition:

7
NOTES, STEMS AND FLAGS

A note has up to three distinct parts:

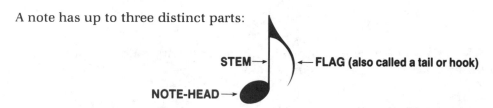

STEM→ ←FLAG (also called a tail or hook)

NOTE-HEAD→

TABLE OF NOTES AND RESTS

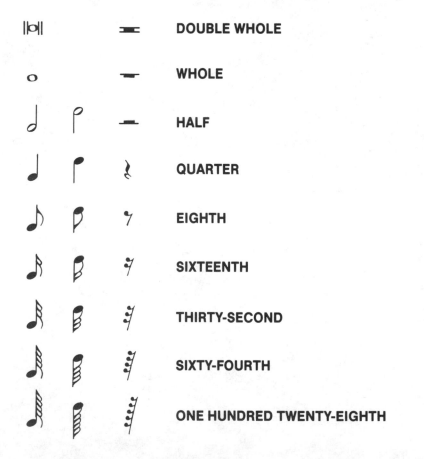

DOUBLE WHOLE

WHOLE

HALF

QUARTER

EIGHTH

SIXTEENTH

THIRTY-SECOND

SIXTY-FOURTH

ONE HUNDRED TWENTY-EIGHTH

7. NOTES, STEMS AND FLAGS

NOTE-HEADS are oval in shape, *not* round. In engraved music, the shading of the whole note differs from the half note and the oval shape may be slightly varied. *Do not attempt to copy these slight differences in manuscript since the absence of a stem is sufficient to distinguish between the two.*

NOTE-HEAD SIZE: Note-heads should always fill a complete space between staff lines, always touching both lines but never overlapping them. Note-heads on staff lines must always be the same size as those which fill spaces. *A common notational error is to carelessly draw note-heads which are too small.*

Cue-size notes are identical to full-size notes except that the proportions of the note-head, stem and flag are equally reduced in size.

UP-STEMS are always attached to the *right* side of note-heads:

DOWN-STEMS are always attached to the *left* side of note-heads:

FLAGS are always placed on the right side of the stem, regardless of stem direction:

STEM DIRECTION ON SINGLE NOTE-HEADS:

Note-heads *below* the center line: **stem up**

Note-heads *on the center line:* **stem up or down**

Note-heads *above* the center line: **stem down**

Engraved examples will usually show stems down on the center line. It is correct, however, to stem them either up or down, depending on the majority stem direction in a given measure.

STEM LENGTH: Stems usually extend up or down one octave from the note-head.

When ledger lines are used, the stems are always extended to touch the center line of the staff. The reason for these longer stems is to accommodate the addition of flags or beams without crossing over or covering the ledger lines:

Note that beams are not angled when all notes are on ledger lines

Stems must be lengthened to accommodate more than one flag or beam:

STEMMING TWO PARTS ON A SINGLE STAFF

Traditional practice dictated that up- and down-stems be used at all times whenever two distinct vocal or instrumental parts shared the same staff. This style is no longer recommended. **When rhythmic values remain generally the same in both parts, common stemming (a single stem for both parts) is preferred:**

PREFERRED: **NOT RECOMMENDED:**

When two parts share the same staff and unison notes are encountered, the unisons should be double-stemmed:

*Two note-heads must be used to clearly indicate whole notes which are in unison.

7. NOTES, STEMS AND FLAGS

Extended unison passages for two parts on a single staff may be single-stemmed if one of the following directives is used:

a2 (Italian abbreviation for *a due*)
> Used in instrumental music to indicate that both instruments play single-stemmed unisons.

Unison or **unis.** (placed above the staff)
> Used in choral music to indicate that all voices are to sing the single-stemmed unisons.

When time values differ on a unison for two instruments or voices, both note values must be shown on the same degree of the staff with separate up- and down-stems. (Whole notes are positioned as though they had stems.) An easily-remembered rule is to *place stem next to stem:*

Exception: When the upper voice is dotted, the note-heads are placed against each other:

Double stemming is obligatory in vocal music when a different text is sung by each part:

Stemming the interval of a second when two parts share the same staff: Some editions use single stems for all seconds and this can lead to confusion. It is strongly recommended that seconds be double-stemmed whenever two parts share a single staff:

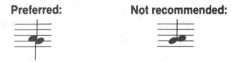

Note the *stem-next-to-stem* placement in the first example above. The alignment of the note-heads is changed when double stemming is used. When seconds are single-stemmed, the higher pitch is always positioned to the right. This "uphill" alignment is always the same when seconds are single-stemmed, regardless of stem direction.

Single stems on seconds are acceptable for keyboard instruments, harp, handbells and those instruments upon which the seconds can be executed by one player.

AUGMENTATION DOTS

The discussion of augmentation dots is often overlooked because their placement seems so elementary. Yet if the novice were asked to dot the note-heads in the interval of seconds shown above, it would probably be done incorrectly. The rules, however, are quite simple.

Single augmentation dots are placed following note-heads and rests to increase their duration by one-half. Double dots increase the duration of notes and rests by three-fourths. (Triple augmentation dots are rarely used; their time values are best indicated through the use of tied notes.)

Dots are always placed in a space and *never* on a line. If a note is on a line, the dot is positioned in the space above, including the dots for notes which are set on ledger lines. When a flagged note must be dotted, the dot is placed beyond the tail of the flag:

Never place two dots for *separate* notes in the same space on the staff. The interval of a second requires placing dots in the spaces above and below the staff line. When a chord contains note clusters, the placement of several dots may have to be adjusted as illustrated:

The following example illustrates the preferred dot placement when two parts share the same staff or when dotted note values differ on the same beat:

7. NOTES, STEMS AND FLAGS

STEM DIRECTION ON CHORDS

The same general rules apply to stemming chords as single notes: **If the majority of the notes in the chord are above the center line, stem down; if most of the notes in the chord are below the center line, stem up:**

ALIGNING THE INTERVAL OF SECONDS WITHIN CHORDS: Seconds are always positioned adjacent to one another, separated by the stem of the chord. The higher pitch is always placed to the right on both up- and down-stems. Whole notes are aligned as if they were stemmed:

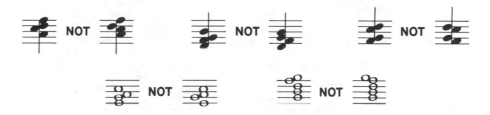

DIFFERENT NOTE VALUES WITHIN A CHORD: When a chord contains a note (or notes) of differing value, the moving note must be stemmed separately and positioned slightly outside the stationary notes:

If the moving note is dotted, it must be placed to the right of the chord so that the dot is immediately adjacent to the note it affects. In other words, a stem must never come between a note and its dot:

8

BEAMS

A series of 8th, 16th, or 32nd notes would be difficult for the eye to organize into metrical units if each had an individual flag as shown in the first example below. To eliminate this confusion, beams replace the flags to visually organize notes into metrical divisions:

The number of beams is equivalent to a like number of flags:

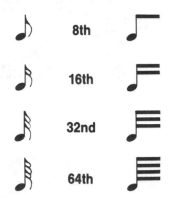

128th notes are rarely used in modern notation.
Note that stems must be longer on notes with more than two flags or beams.

Beams are considerably thicker than stems and care must be taken in manuscript preparation to draw them correctly. A ruler is essential for drawing all but the shortest beams and a second pencil stroke is required to achieve proper beam thickness.

8. BEAMS

A PRIMARY BEAM takes the place of individual flags and connects all of the stems, forming a unit of 8th notes:

SECONDARY BEAMS represent the additional flags of shorter value notes. These secondary beams connect only with the stems of the notes they affect. Stems are always drawn *through* secondary beams to connect with the primary beam:

SHORT SECONDARY BEAMS are used with dotted note values included in beamed units. The short secondary beam must be placed *under* the primary beam, never outside the note-grouping. It always faces the direction of the dot(s). A secondary beam must be drawn as thick as the primary beam. If the edge of the short beam is not squared off, it can easily be mistaken for a poorly-written note-head:

Beaming in Triple Meter

Any number of beats *may* be beamed together in triple meter because there is only one strong pulse in a measure. For example, all six 8th notes in a measure of $\frac{3}{4}$ time could be beamed together *or* in groups of two:

When note values in $\frac{3}{4}$ are mixed, it becomes obvious that each beat should be beamed separately:

Measures containing only dotted quarter notes and 8th notes are much easier to read when all 8th notes are beamed as a single unit:

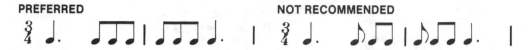

PREFERRED   NOT RECOMMENDED

Beaming in Duple Meter

One or two beats may be beamed together in duple meter. Since any measure in duple meter can be equally divided in two, there is a natural division (or secondary pulse) which usually is not covered by a beam. In other words, all beaming is usually separated ahead of the natural division of the measure. There are exceptions, such as beaming a recurring rhythmical pattern, but the secondary pulse in duple meter is generally left "open" and a beam is not drawn over it.

In $\frac{4}{4}$, a series of 8th notes would logically be beamed in units of four, with the natural division on the third beat remaining uncovered:

UNCOVERED

In $\frac{4}{4}$, when note values are shorter than 8ths or when note values are mixed, beam in units which distinctly show all four beats:

Beaming across bar lines is permissible to organize rhythmic patterns or syncopations:

The notator will soon discover many situations where unusual beaming is required and it would be impossible to show all such examples here. A study of complex piano or harp editions will best serve as reference to illustrate many beaming options available in complicated notation.

8. BEAMS

BEAM PLACEMENT AND DIRECTION

The placement of beams is governed by the general direction of stems in the group of notes to be beamed. If most of the stems in the grouping go up, then all of the stems are drawn upward and the beam is placed above. The opposite is true if the majority of the stems go downward:

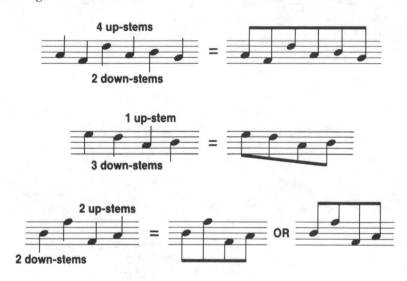

The angle of the beam is determined by the general contour and/or overall balance of the note-heads as shown:

The beam remains horizontal for groups of alternating notes and for note groupings which begin and end on the same degree of the staff:

TYPICAL BEAMING PATTERNS

There are probably as many exceptions as there are rules when it comes to beaming, particularly in keyboard notation. **The following examples are all correct** but it is immediately apparent that different beaming patterns can greatly facilitate reading. Simply remember that the primary function of beaming is visual organization.

9
IRREGULAR NOTE GROUPINGS

Duplets, triplets, quintuplets and other irregular note groupings require special discussion. Even music engravers and publishers are inconsistent in the elements of notating irregular note groupings, yet there are some basic rules which should be followed.

When an irregular note grouping is used, a numeral is employed to indicate the number of notes in the group. When these note values are beamed with up-stems, the numeral is centered over the beam which unites the grouping. When the notes are down-stemmed, the numeral is centered beneath the beam:

When an irregular note grouping is repeated consecutively, the numeral is usually shown only with the first two groupings, followed by the directive *simile:*

A square bracket* must be used to unite groupings of notes which are not joined with a beam. The bracket is placed over or under the stems and the numeral must be included with the bracket. The numeral may be positioned in one of two ways:

The bracket is slanted to follow the direction of the notes within it, just as a beam would be slanted if it were used.

---

*A curved slur is sometimes used instead of the square bracket. The bracket is preferred.

The bracket is also required if the grouping contains both flagged and unflagged notes:

Note that the numeral should be placed between the notes and not in the middle of the rhythmic center when groupings contain two differing note values.

When rests form a part of a grouping (whether beamed or not), a bracket is required if a rest is at the beginning or end of the figure:

The bracket is not required when a beam *covers* rests:

9. IRREGULAR NOTE GROUPINGS

NOTE VALUES FOR IRREGULAR GROUPINGS

Confusion sets in when trying to determine note values for many irregular groupings. For example, a scale passage of seven notes must be set against a single quarter note. Should that septuplet be beamed as 16th or 32nd notes?

The table below illustrates the note values for irregular groupings when the quarter note is in the basic unit. (The regular groupings of 8ths, 16ths and 32nds are included to show at a glance how their number of beams relate to the irregular groupings.)

WHEN NOTATING THIS NUMBER OF NOTES AGAINST A QUARTER:	BEAM THE GROUPING AS:	COMMON NAME
2	8th NOTES	Duplet
3	↓	Triplet
4	16th NOTES	Quadruplet
5	↓	Quintuplet
6	↓	Sextuplet
7	↓	Septuplet
8	32nd NOTES	Octuplet
9	↓	Nonuplet
10	↓	Decuplet
11 *through* 15	↓	*No common names*
16	64th NOTES	↓
17 *through* 31	↓	↓

The most common of irregular note-groupings is three against two. **The note values of the triplet and the duplet are always the same:**

While any combination of unequal groups is possible, notators will rarely have to set nonuplets, decuplets or other irregular groupings against a common duplet. Hence, the following are representative of the examples most commonly encountered:

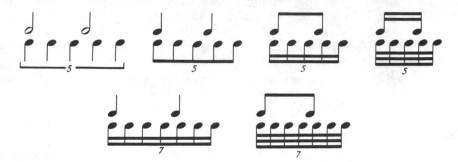

COMPOUND METERS ($\frac{6}{8}$, $\frac{9}{8}$ and $\frac{12}{8}$): Three eighth-notes comprise one beat and a duplet would therefore be an irregular note grouping. Duplets may be notated in two ways:

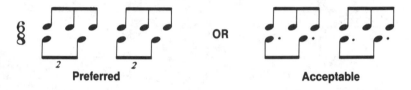

A five-note grouping (quintuplet) is also written in eighth notes:

A seven-note grouping (septuplet) is notated in 16th notes:

10
ACCIDENTALS

Accidentals are the symbols placed directly in front of note-heads to indicate chromatic alterations or to cancel them. The same symbols are used in key signatures but the term *accidental* refers specifically to these signs when they are applied to individual notes.

All five accidentals are easy to draw and they should be written in close approximation to their engraved form:

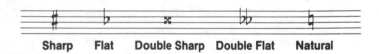

Sharp   Flat   Double Sharp   Double Flat   Natural

Note carefully that portion of each accidental which completely fills the space between staff lines. When accidentals are placed on the lines themselves, observe the same proportions.

An accidental affects the note immediately following and those on the same degree of the staff within the measure. Accidentals do not alter the pitch in different octaves.

CAUTIONARY ACCIDENTALS may be used as performance "reminders." Even though the bar line itself cancels all accidentals from the previous measure (unless they are tied), it is advisable to use cautionary accidentals where there is any chance of doubt. Such reminders are especially appropriate where many accidentals used within a measure might lead to confusion or where an altered note is tied over a page-turn.

Cautionary accidentals have traditionally been enclosed in parentheses, in addition to sometimes being drawn much smaller (cue-size). This practice is questionable, if for no other reason than the unnecessary clutter which the parentheses add to the score. Modern editions usually omit the parentheses and use full-size cautionary accidentals.

Cue-size cautionary accidentals placed above the staff, over the note and its stem, are occasionally encountered but the most pragmatic approach is recommended: ***when a cautionary accidental is required, use a full-size symbol without parentheses and place it directly in front of the note-head.***

REPEATED ACCIDENTALS within a measure are obligatory for vocal and instrumental music when two parts share the same staff; any pitch altered by an accidental must show the accidental a second time if another voice subsequently moves to that pitch:

ALIGNMENT OF ACCIDENTALS

Established patterns should be observed whenever aligning accidentals with the notes of a chord:

TWO NOTES SHARING THE SAME STEM: Always draw the uppermost accidental first, placing it close to the note-head. The accidental for the bottom note is placed slightly to the left of the first accidental if the interval is smaller than a seventh. If the interval is larger than a seventh, the accidentals should be aligned vertically:

CHORDS OF THREE NOTES: If three accidentals are needed, place the uppermost accidental first, closest to the note-head. The accidental for the middle note is shifted to the left, allowing space for the third accidental to be centered between the two which were drawn first:

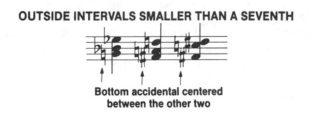

The top and bottom accidentals are aligned vertically if the interval between these notes is a seventh or larger. The accidental for the middle note is still shifted to the left:

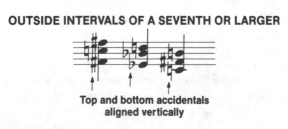

10. ACCIDENTALS

CHORDS OF FOUR OR MORE NOTES: When four or more accidentals are required, draw the uppermost accidental first, closest to the note-head. The accidental for the bottom note is usually drawn next and in most cases the interval will be a seventh or more, allowing it to be aligned vertically with the top accidental. The placement of accidentals between the top and bottom may vary and the notator must make adjustments to the normal left/right patterns.

Regardless of the number of accidentals, they should never be crowded, nor should any accidental be drawn smaller or with shortened vertical lines merely to fit it into place. The lines of accidentals never cross one another. Always leave ample space so that all accidentals may be arranged in a diagonal pattern, even if some of the symbols appear at some distance from the notes they affect:

When double stemming is used on a single staff, accidentals should not be placed between the up- and down-stems. They are always drawn in front of the entire unit:

11

RESTS

It would seem logical that rests and notes of the same value could be substituted for one another, but this is not always the case. For example, the half rest is never used in $\frac{3}{4}$ meter, even though it is the equivalent of two quarter rests. (Half rests may be substituted for two quarter rests only if a measure can be equally divided in half. Certain other exceptions are discussed throughout this section.)

WHOLE RESTS

Whole rests (which also serve as measure rests) differ from all other rests in their placement: they are always *centered* in the measure. In modern notation, the whole rest is used exclusively to represent an entire measure and never a fraction thereof. Whole rests are normally placed beneath the fourth staff line; think of them as "hanging" from the fourth staff line:

When two parts are written on the same staff, whole rests are usually placed beneath the top and bottom staff lines:

When space on the staff does not permit the placement shown above, ledger lines may be used instead, either above or below the staff:

---

*The double whole rest, though rare in modern notation, shares the same positioning as the whole rest.

11. RESTS

With the exception of the whole rest, **the placement of all other rests is identical to the placement of their corresponding note values.** In other words, rests are positioned precisely on the *beginning* of the beat and never centered in the space which a beat may occupy.

HALF RESTS

Half rests are always placed on the *beginning* of the beat, precisely where a half *note* would be placed. *It is incorrect to center half rests in the space they fill.* Placement is usually *on* the third line of the staff; think of them as "sitting" on this line:

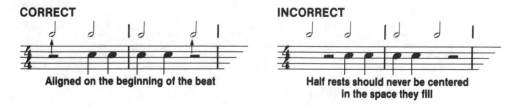

When two parts share the same staff, half rests are positioned "sitting" on the top and bottom lines of the staff:

Ledger lines may be used if space does not permit placement on the top and bottom staff lines:

Half rests are never used in $\frac{3}{4}$ meter. Two quarter rests must be used instead:

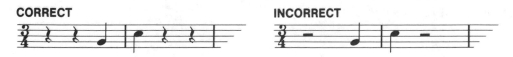

ALL OTHER RESTS

Rests from the quarter through the 8th, 16th, 32nd, etc., are normally centered vertically on the staff between the top and bottom staff lines. Observe the positioning of the hooks on the rests of shorter duration:

QUARTER 8th   16th   32nd   64th   128th

If two parts share the same staff, their rests are usually placed above and below the center staff line. When space prohibits this placement, the rests may even fall totally above or below the staff:

Rests should not obscure the normal pulse division of the measure in duple meter:

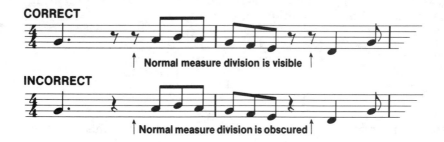

DOTTED RESTS

Rests may be dotted just as notes are dotted. The dot increases the value of the rest by one-half. Double dots may also be used with rests. (Triple dots are theoretically possible but inadvisable.)

11. RESTS

MULTIPLE-MEASURE RESTS

Rests which encompass many measures are used in instrumental or choral parts which are separate from the full score. These multiple-measure rests may be used to count off any number of measures (above two) if no rehearsal letter, change of tempo, fermata, pause, etc., occur. If any of these elements are present, the multiple-measure rest must be terminated to show the exact location of such features in the score.

Multiple-measure rests take on many written forms, especially in manuscript, but the most common is the heavy bar placed on the middle line of the staff as shown below. The centered numeral indicates the number of full measures of rest. *Note some of the elements which must not be obscured by these extended rests:*

IMPORTANT: The fermata ⌢ and break // symbols should be placed precisely on the same beat in all parts. The conductor and performers must know which beat is prolonged or where a break occurs. For example, a fermata should never be placed over a whole note or whole rest in one part and over the last quarter note in other parts. Note also that inverted fermatas placed beneath down-stems are usually unnecessary and redundant.

12

TIES AND SLURS

A tie connects two successive notes of identical pitch, uniting them and combining their durations. Tie marks should be drawn to the center of the note-heads but should not actually touch them. This is illustrated in many examples which follow.

PLACEMENT AND DIRECTION OF TIES

SINGLE NOTES with up-stems: Tie curves below
            with down-stems: Tie curves above

Position ties on single whole notes as if they were stemmed

TWO NOTES with common stem: Tie upper note above
                           Tie lower note below

THREE NOTES with common stem: Tie upper note above
                            Tie lower note below
Inner tie: curves above if note is high on the staff
         curves below if note is low on the staff

FOUR TIED NOTES with common stem:
        Tie upper two notes above
        Tie lower two notes below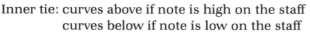

FIVE OR MORE TIED NOTES with common stem:
        Tie upper two notes above
        Tie lower two notes below
        Tie middle notes: above if high on the staff
                     below if low on the staff

12. TIES AND SLURS

Since ties should never be drawn *through* note-heads, there will be exceptions to the above guidelines and an explicit visual approach must be substituted. *Ties may be drawn through stems but never through beams or other symbols.* If symbols such as clef signs or time signatures obstruct the placement of ties, the ties may be broken on either side of such symbols:

Ties which continue to the next system should not extend beyond the end of the staff and into the right margin. Such ties correctly terminate just inside the bar line at the end of each line.

INCOMPLETE TIES

Short, incomplete ties are sometimes used over successive bar lines and the note-heads themselves omitted completely if the tied notes remain unchanged and the measures are especially wide. The final tied notes should be shown with their precise values:

Incomplete ties are also used for instruments with long sustaining capabilities (such as handbells, harp or piano) to indicate that the notes so marked should be allowed to fade into silence. The abbreviation **L.V.** or **l.v.** (for the French *laissez vibrer*, easily remembered in English as "let vibrate") is sometimes used as a directive at the first occurrence of incomplete ties.

L. V. (or l. v.)

SLURS

The slur and the tie are identical marks but they serve totally different purposes. This dual-purpose mark must therefore be precisely positioned in manuscript work to avoid confusion.

Slurs have been used in music notation for centuries, with totally different meanings or interpretations along the way. One of the most common uses of the slur in modern practice is to indicate melodic phrases or to visually unify groupings of notes. Both applications, unfortunately, are misused and result in unnecessary clutter. Composers often add slurs to the page much like the diner who salts his food before tasting it.

If the composer's intent is a *legato* style, would it not reduce clutter to simply include the directive *sempre legato* (or perhaps more succinctly, *smoothly*)? Will not the sensitive performer consider phrasing a matter of interpretation and tend to ignore overabundant slurs anyway?

When the composer or notator wishes to indicate preferred or unusual phrasing, slurs should be added judiciously. Remember that one insertion of the word *simile* can be used to eliminate redundant slurs after a pattern has been established.

VOCAL SLURS are mandatory when one word or syllable is extended over many notes. Some modern editions have eliminated vocal slurs on all notes which are beamed but this is a questionable reform. Singers prefer a visual grouping of notes on all mellismatic passages. **INSTRUMENTAL SLURS** may be used for wind instruments to indicate tonguing; they also show bowing patterns for strings.

BROKEN SLURS (sometimes called dotted slurs) are used in vocal music to indicate "no breath."

PLACEMENT OF SLURS

The preferred placement of slurs is over or under the *note-heads*. Since stem directions change constantly, placement must often be altered with slurs being drawn over (but not *through*) some stems, flags or beams:

12. TIES AND SLURS

Slurs should always be drawn accurately to "enclose" note groupings, never casually dangling in space. It is again emphasized that precise placement is absolutely necessary to avoid any confusion between slur marks and ties:

Vague and unacceptable slur placement

If a slurred passage ends with tied notes, the slur must extend beyond these ties to include the final *notes:*

CORRECT　　　　　　　　　　　　　**INCORRECT**

Slurs should not be drawn *through* any symbols other than bar lines. In rare instances, a slur may be broken to accommodate another symbol, continuing thereafter. This can usually be avoided if the layout is planned in advance.

In conclusion, when the need for slurs is unquestionable, use them. Otherwise, keep their use to a minimum.

13
ACCENTS

Symbols used to indicate various forms of articulation are all categorized as accent marks. All of these accent markings should be placed directly above or below the note heads, the only exception being the sforzato (Λ) as noted below. These symbols should follow the general rise and fall of the note-heads but should never be written across the staff itself (with the exception of the *staccato* and *tenuto* marks).

When space does not permit accent marks to be placed next to the note-heads, the symbols may be inserted over beams, flags, and stems.

Only *staccato* and *tenuto* marks may be written on the spaces of the staff:

13. ACCENTS

The principal accents marks shown below usually stand alone, although some symbols are occasionally combined. The interpretation of combined symbols becomes one of considerable debate and a subject beyond the scope of this book. Accent marks may take on dissimilar meanings when applied to voices or different instruments.

 This accent mark is the most common. It always "points" in the same direction and is never written <. The symbol has several Italian names, all variants of *rinforzando;* in English it is called simply an *accent* or *accent mark.*

 The *sforzato* or *forzando* is the heaviest of percussive accents and **the only one written above or below the stem.** (This symbol is inverted when placed below the stem.) A darker line shades one side of this symbol.

 The *staccato* dot is placed immediately above or below the note-head and it is written on the spaces of the staff if the note-head placement so allows.

 Used to indicate *martellato,* hammered or strongly marked. This symbol is never inverted.

 The short, bold dash is called a *tenuto* mark. It is placed immediately above or below the note-head and is written on the spaces of the staff if the note-head placement so allows. This mark is peculiarly subject to different interpretations but the most universally accepted is that of giving full value to the note, sometimes even slightly prolonging it. In organ music, the mark indicates a distinct separation of successive notes, i.e., well-marked. In vocal music it can indicate a subtle stress. The notator is cautioned to apply this mark with prudence.

Notators are reminded that too many successive accent marks often lose visual impact. Once an accented pattern has been established, the insertion of *simile* eliminates the need for additional accents, greatly reducing clutter.

NOMENCLATURE USED FOR ACCENTS

Several Italian words are abbreviated to indicate additional forms of accent. These abbreviations (not the full words) are generally used to imply that one particular chord or note is played with great force or emphasis:

> **sf** or **sfz** = *sforzando*
> **fz** or **ffz** = *forzando* or *forzato*
>
> **sfp** = played *sforzando* but suddenly diminishing to *piano*.
>   Common in brass notation for dramatic, percussive effects.
>
> *Additional forte marks added to the above abbreviations*
> *(as **sfffz**) are sometimes used but considered superfluous.*

It is often preferable to use simple English rather than an endless string of accent marks to convey a style of performance. Directives such as *slightly detached* or *strongly accented* or *heavily* are concise and convincing.

14

ORNAMENTS

The vast number of ornaments once used (and variously interpreted) in music notation has been reduced to but a few in music of the 20th century. Today's notator is advised to avoid embellishments such as the mordent, turn, double appoggiatura and the like since these obscure symbols will leave interpretation open to speculation and chance. It is far better to notate every embellishment in full.

TRILL

The trill is notated with the abbreviation **tr** [no period] placed over the staff, directly above the principal note. A horizontal wavy line is usually drawn after the sign for all but the shortest trills:

A trill which covers several measures is shown in notes which are tied, with the wavy line extending unbroken over the entire unit:

A trill is always executed with the secondary note being the diatonic scale step above the written note. An accidental must be included if the secondary note is other than diatonic:

Note: The **tr** symbol is also used to indicate a roll on timpani and all *unpitched* percussion instruments, even though it is not actually a trill in the literal sense.

GRACE NOTES

Notes not counted in the rhythm of the measure are commonly called grace notes or appoggiaturas. Like most ornaments, grace notes are subject to more than one interpretation. In early music, the appoggiatura was always accented, *on* the beat, but in modern music it is usually unaccented.

Single grace notes are written as small (cue-size) eighth notes with a slash drawn through the stem and flag. Two or three grace notes are joined with two beams; four or more are usually drawn with three beams. A slur is commonly drawn to unite the grace note(s) to the first note of the beat which follows:

All grace notes must be written ahead of the beat with stems drawn upward, regardless of the note positions on the staff.

ARPEGGIATED CHORDS

The arpeggio symbol (a vertical wavy line drawn in front of a chord) indicates that the notes of the chord are to be rolled from the bottom to the top.

An arrow should never be placed at the top of this symbol.

A downward arpeggio uses the same wavy line and placement but with an added arrowhead at the bottom of the sign, indicating that the notes are to be rolled from the top to the bottom:

14. ORNAMENTS

The arpeggio symbol in keyboard music may be interpreted in two ways:

A continuous, unbroken wavy line drawn in front of the chords and *between* the two staves indicates that the notes are rolled successively from the bottom note of the left hand to the top note of the right hand.

When the wavy line is *broken* between the staves, both chords are rolled simultaneously.

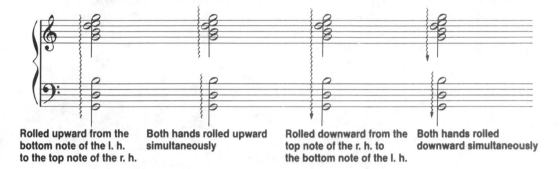

Rolled upward from the bottom note of the l. h. to the top note of the r. h.

Both hands rolled upward simultaneously

Rolled downward from the top note of the r. h. to the bottom note of the l. h.

Both hands rolled downward simultaneously

Note: In harp music, chords of more than two notes are *always* rolled or slightly broken unless a square bracket [is placed in front of the note-heads. The arpeggio symbol is therefore used only to indicate a downward arpeggio (with the added arrow) or drawn unbroken between the staves to indicate an arpeggio rolled through with both hands from the bottom to the top note.

TREMOLO

The term *tremolo* has several different meanings. With stringed instruments, for example, it indicates a quick reiteration of the same tone which may also be measured—a subject beyond the scope of this book. The *unmeasured* tremolo, used by many differing instruments, is discussed here and referred to simply as *tremolo*.

The tremolo is generally thought of as a rapid alternation of two notes. Two beams are used to join two notes *of the same value* to indicate a tremolo. (In very slow tempos, three beams may be used.) In other words, if a tremolo is to fill four beats in $\frac{4}{4}$ meter, the whole-note values are duplicated on the two tones to be employed. Shown below are common examples of note values which must be used to fill an entire measure in the meters indicated:

Placement of the second note of the tremolo is always precisely in the center of the metrical unit.

Rules governing tremolo beams:

> Whole notes obviously cannot be physically joined; the beams must be drawn between them.
>
> Beams on quarter notes are not connected to the stems (to avoid the appearance of sixteenth notes).
>
> Secondary beams on eighth notes are not connected to the stems (to avoid mistaking them as sixteenth notes). Although uncommon, tremolos shown with shorter value notes must also have disconnected secondary beams to eliminate confusion.

GLISSANDO

A glissando is indicated with a straight line drawn from the starting note to the note on which it terminates. The abbreviation **gliss.** may be inserted above or below the angled line. Since a glissando can be executed at various speeds, the duration is governed by the value of the starting note; the glissando then terminates on the beat indicated by the concluding note:

In very slow passages, a short glissando covering few notes should usually be written out in full note values since such a figure would probably require individual fingering.

The notator is cautioned to make a specialized study of harp before attempting to write glissandi for this instrument since pedal settings must always be indicated.

15
DYNAMIC MARKINGS AND DIRECTIVES

The dynamic markings used in music are all based on abbreviations of Italian terms:

m = *mezzo* (medium)
p = *piano* (soft)
f = *forte* (loud)

mf and *mp* are considered the middle of a dynamic range
extending from the softest to the loudest

Extremes such as ***PPPPPP*** *(pianississississississimo)* or ***ffffff*** *(fortisississississimo)* may be shown on paper but are totally unrealistic. The practical dynamic range is best limited to the following scale:

MINIMUM ←——————————————→ **MAXIMUM**
pppp   ppp   pp   p   mp   mf   f   ff   fff   ffff

Three additional Italian abbreviations also serve as important dynamic markings. These abbreviations or their equivalent symbols (called *hairpins* or *wedges)* are synonymous:

cresc. *(crescendo)* = gradually louder

decres. *(decrescendo)* or **dim.** *(diminuendo)* = gradually softer

The terms *diminuendo* and *decrescendo* are synonymous.

The abbreviations or symbols for *crescendo* or *diminuendo* should never stand alone. They must always be followed by a dynamic marking to clearly indicate the desired volume level to be attained. Printed editions often show a crescendo or diminuendo with no concluding dynamic level indicated but this represents only carelessness. The performer must know how loud or how soft the change in dynamics is to become:

*The prevailing dynamic level would obviously be shown in the manuscript well ahead of any change.

HAIRPINS (WEDGES) may often interfere with other symbols. While hairpins may be drawn through stems, it is generally inadvisable to do so. (Any symbol which is drawn through another tends to clutter the score.) The best solution in crowded situations is to substitute the abbreviation **cresc., dim.,** or **decresc.** All three of these abbreviations may be modified with **poco** (meaning "little") or **molto** (meaning "much" or "considerable").

Modifiers such as *poco* or *molto* may not always convey the desired intent. While Italian was once considered the universal language in music, English may be even more universally understood today. For that reason, many composers and notators prefer to use simple English in certain situations. However, be consistent and do not carelessly intermix the two languages. *Gradual cresc.* is inappropriate and redundant; *gradually louder* is correct and better serves the purpose. Longer directives such as *poco a poco diminuendo al fine* may be proper but *gradually fading to the end* commands immediate comprehension, especially if the score will be read by amateur musicians.

PLACEMENT OF DYNAMIC MARKINGS

Keyboard music: Place dynamic markings between the staves when dynamics are the same for both hands. When the dynamic level between the two hands is different, place dynamic markings above or below each staff.

Instrumental music: Dynamic markings are placed below the staff. If two instruments share the same staff, the dynamic markings are placed above and below the staff when dynamic levels differ.

Vocal music: Dynamic markings are commonly placed above the staff. If two parts are written on the same staff, differing dynamic levels are be indicated above and below that staff.

16

REPETITION SIGNS

Repetition signs fall into two categories: those used primarily as shorthand in manuscript, and the standard signs used in engraved scores (which are obviously used in manuscript as well).

STANDARD ENGRAVED SYMBOLS

REPEAT SIGNS: Repeated sections of more than two measures are set off between repeat signs (a symbol similar in appearance to a final double bar line but with double dots added). Note how the symbol is reversed at the beginning and end of the repeat:

Repeat signs may be placed on any beat within a measure and they need not always serve as regular bar lines:

> The above form can be useful when a repeated section must include an incomplete measure at the beginning of a composition. However, in most instances it is preferable to write out full measures to avoid possible confusion.

Sections may be repeated back-to-back, using a modified repeat sign between the two:

Note that if a repeat sign is shown only at the end, the repetition is to start from the beginning of the composition. In other words, **do not place a repeat sign at the beginning of a composition when the repeat commences on the opening beat of the first measure.**

FIRST AND SECOND ENDINGS are often used in conjunction with a repeated section. More than two endings may also be indicated. They are numbered consecutively; a **Final ending** may also be used. The different forms of these endings is illustrated below; the horizontal bracket above the staff is "closed" with a downstroke on all but the last ending in each example. This final bracket is always left "open" where it terminates after being drawn above one full measure:

Note the form for continuing a first ending at the end of a system:

If the first ending is to be used more than once, the number of repetitions is shown in numerals within the bracket of the first ending to read **1., 2.** [or more], indicating this ending is used the first *and* second [or more] times. The **3.** [insert correct sequence number] is then shown under the second bracket to serve as the last ending of the repeated sequence.

Note that all first and second (or multiple) endings must be shown above the uppermost staff of each part included in a system.

The thoughtful notator will give attention to convenient page-turns in the middle of a repeat if the manuscript is to be used in performances. When necessary, leave blank staves at the bottom of a page (marked over with a broad, wavy line) to facilitate difficult page-turns.

16. REPETITION SIGNS

DA CAPO and **DAL SEGNO:** Abbreviations of Italian terms are used to indicate the repeat of extended sections within a composition:

D.C. *(da capo)* = from the beginning
D.S. *(dal segno)* = from the sign 𝄋

The **D.C.** or **D.S.** abbreviation is placed above the top staff of each instrumental or vocal part in the score, immediately ahead of the bar line where the repeat takes place. These abbreviations are often modified with additional directives as shown below:

D.C. indicates a repeat from the very beginning, then continuing to the end (marked by a final double bar line). The D.C. may be placed anywhere within the composition, although it most frequently appears at the end.

D.S. al Fine indicates a repeat from the very beginning and continuing to the point where the word **Fine** appears in the score above a final double bar line.

D.C. al Coda (sometimes written **D.C. al segno e poi la Coda**) indicates a repeat from the very beginning to the sign ⊕ which indicates a skip to the **Coda** (which is usually marked with the sign ⊕).

D.S. indicates a repeat back to the sign 𝄋 , then continuing to the end (marked by a final double bar line). The D.S. may be placed anywhere within the composition although it most frequently appears at the end.

D.S. al Fine indicates a repeat back to the sign 𝄋 , then continuing to where the word **Fine** appears in the score above a final double bar line.

OTHER USEFUL REPETITION SIGNS

The following repetition signs are used primarily in manuscript; however, they also appear in engraved instrumental parts. Since these signs are seldom used in keyboard music, the notator is cautioned to use them only where appropriate.

MEASURE REPEAT: Used to indicate the exact repetition of an entire measure. This symbol may also be used to show consecutive repeats of a single measure. The addition of numerals facilitates counting the repetitions. (The numeral **1** is not shown since it represents the measure being repeated.)

TWO-MEASURE REPEAT: The measure repeat sign is centered over the bar line to indicate that two full measures are to be repeated; the numeral **2** should be added above the symbol, over the bar line, to emphasize that it is a two-measure repeat.

For more than two repeated measures use the standard repeat bars described at the beginning of this section.

A REPEATED BEAT may be indicated with a heavy slash mark positioned as shown below. This single slash mark may be used for repeated quarter notes or eighth notes.

Two slash marks, drawn close together, are used to represent repeated sixteenth notes; three slash marks for thirty-second notes, etc.

When preparing a manuscript for engraving, the copyist should use colored pencil to clearly highlight any repetition symbols which the engraver is expected to write out in full and also write specific directions in the margin on such pages.

In conclusion, it must be emphasized that while repetition signs save copying time, they must never confuse the performer. Any shorthand which might be misread should be written out in full.

INDEX